D1432707

Fire stations house fire trucks, firefighters, and gear

FIELD TRIPS

A Fire Station

Jill Kalz

A+
Smart Apple Media

COPYRIGHT

For my dad, Roger Kalz, New Ulm Fire Department, 1975–96

Published by Smart Apple Media
1980 Lookout Drive, North Mankato, MN 56003
Designed by Rita Marshall

Printed in the United States of America

Photographs by Image Finders (Jeff Greenberg, Patti McConville, T. Williams, Jim Yokajty), Jeff Myers, Tom Myers, Unicorn Stock Photos (Aneal Vohra)

Library of Congress Cataloging-in-Publication Data
Kalz, Jill. A fire station / by Jill Kalz.
p. cm. – (Field trips) Includes bibliographical references and index.
Summary: Briefly describes what goes on at a fire station, the people who work there either as professional or volunteer firefighters, the equipment they use, and what happens when a fire alarm is sounded. Includes a related activity.
ISBN 1-58340-326-4
1. Fire stations–Juvenile literature. 2. Fire extinction–Juvenile literature.
[1. Fire stations.] I. Title. II. Field trips (Smart Apple Media) (Mankato, Minn.).
TH9148.K355 2003 628.9'25–dc21 2002042784

First Edition 9 8 7 6 5 4 3 2 1

CONTENTS

A Fire Station

Under the Roof

The garage doors go up. Sirens wail. Red lights flash as the fire trucks rumble into the night. For a while, the fire station will sit empty and quiet. But when the trucks return, the station will once again come to life. A fire station is a building that holds trucks, tools, **turnout gear**, and firefighters. Large cities have many stations, while small towns usually have just one. Some towns even share a fire station, especially in farming areas. All fire stations have a

Firefighters may be called out any time, day or night

garage. Trucks, tools, and gear are stored in the garage. They are kept ready to go at any time to put out a fire. In the rest of the station, there may be an exercise room, a kitchen, offices, or a TV room. There may be a training room, where firefighters take classes to learn new skills or brush up on old skills. Some fire stations have locker rooms, a laundry room, or sleeping rooms with rows of beds.

Not all of the firefighters in the United States are men. Cities started hiring women firefighters in 1974.

Fighting fires is hot, dirty, tiring, and very rewarding

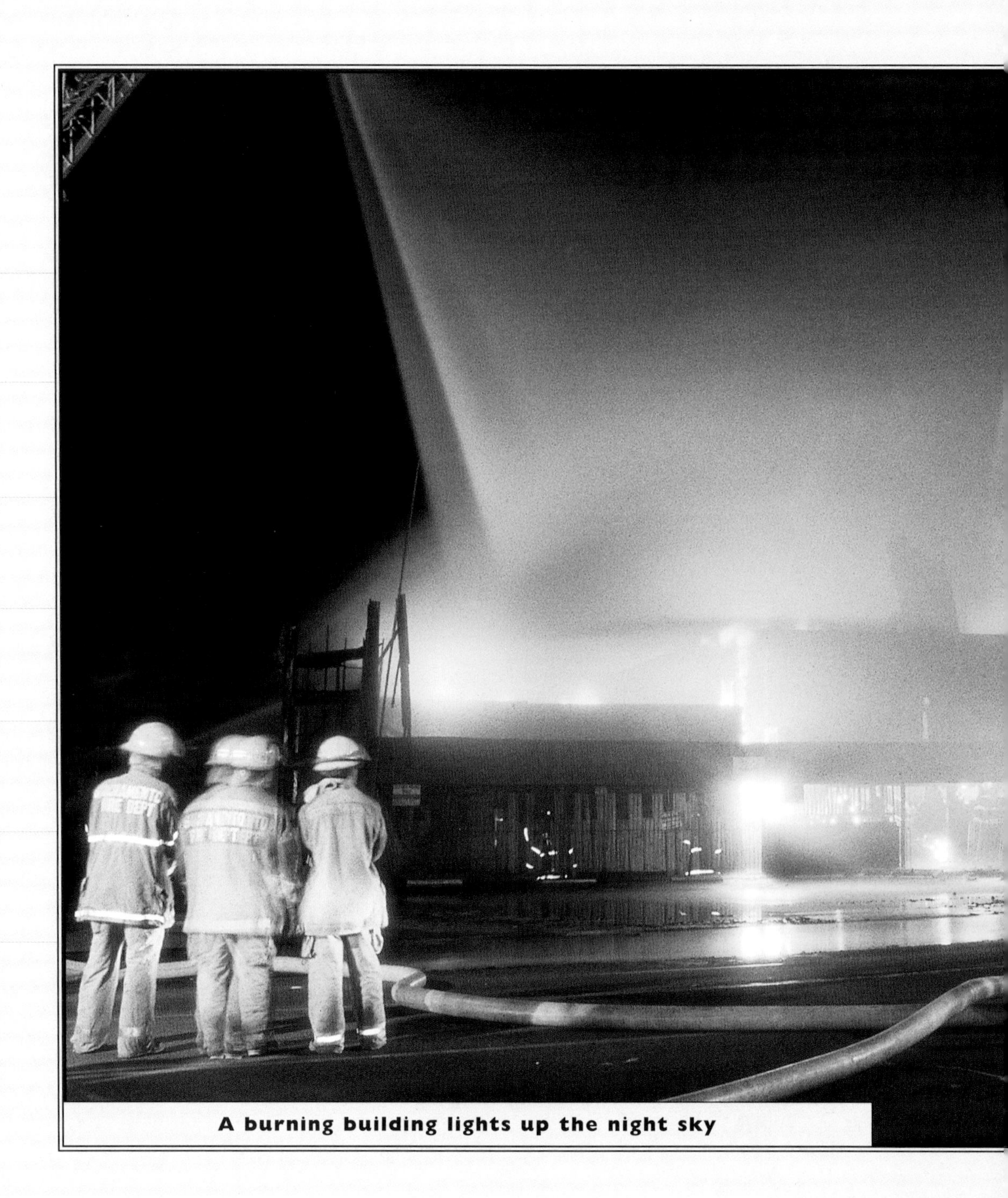

A burning building lights up the night sky

SACRAMENTO
SACRAMENTO
FIRE DEPT.

The Firefighters

Some firefighters live at the fire station for a few days each week. Firefighting is their full-time job. As soon as they walk into the station, they are "on call." They must be ready at any time, even in the middle of the night. Firefighters in big cities may go on more than a dozen **calls** in one day. But they have plenty to do at the station, too. Firefighters wash and repair their trucks. They clean and check their tools and gear. Some of them write reports, buy

Most fire trucks are red. But some fire departments paint their trucks lime green or yellow.

groceries, or cook. Small towns often cannot afford to pay firefighters. There are also fewer fires, so full-time firefighters are not needed. Townspeople may **volunteer** to

It is important to keep fire trucks in good condition

be firefighters. Volunteer firefighters may be doctors, teachers, factory workers, or farmers. Anyone who is in good health and can do the job well can be a volunteer firefighter.

Trucks, Tools, and Gear

Fire stations have at least one of the four kinds of fire trucks: pumper, tanker, ladder, and rescue. Pumpers are the first trucks to leave the station. They carry some water and all of the hoses. The pumpers usually pump water from **fire hydrants**. If there are no hydrants, firefighters use tankers. Holding thousands of gallons of water, tankers dump their

load into portable pools. Then they go refill their tanks. Pumpers use the water in the pools to put out the fire. They can also pump water out of lakes or rivers. The built-in

Water is pumped from a fire hydrant through a hose

ladders on most ladder trucks can reach the top of a 10-story building. Ladder trucks also carry tools that help firefighters break windows and knock down walls to get to a fire. Rescue trucks carry the tools firefighters need to rescue people. They may carry first-aid kits, ropes, axes, metal cutters, spotlights, saws, and much more. Turnout gear helps protect firefighters from danger. Gear includes boots, **bunker pants**, coats, gloves, fireproof hoods, and helmets. Firefighters may also wear air packs and face masks to help them breathe.

Horses once lived in fire stations, too. They were used to pull the fire equipment.

Full turnout gear weighs about 65 pounds (29 kg). Firefighters must be very strong to run, climb, and fight fires in all that heavy gear.

Gushing water can make a fire hose difficult to hold

A Fire Call

When a 911 call comes into the fire station, a **dispatcher** sounds the alarm. Because volunteer firefighters do not live at the station, they carry pagers. Pagers beep to tell volunteers when there is a call. Many stations have fire poles. Sliding down a pole is much faster than taking the stairs. The first person to the garage opens the doors. Then the firefighters put on their gear. Bunker pants are stored with the legs rolled down around the firefighters' boots.

Some old fire stations have been turned into museums, offices, shops, restaurants, and even homes.

Firefighters just step in and pull up! A driver jumps into each truck and starts the engine. The other firefighters climb in back. Many times, firefighters do not know what the call will

Face masks and air packs offer protection from smoke

be like until they get there. It may be a car accident, a barn fire, or just a smoking toaster. Firefighters have to be ready for anything. Each call they get could mean someone's life.

A fire station is more than just a building. For many firefighters, it is their second home. Filled with life-saving tools, shiny trucks, and people who keep us safe, a fire station is an exciting place to visit.

Small towns may average 100 calls per year. New York City averages 350,000.

Firefighters may be kept very busy in large cities

ONE WAY
NO TURN ON RED
PMI
PARK
P
D.F.D.
114

Family Fire Drill

Do you know what to do if a fire breaks out where you live? This activity will help you plan.

What You Need

Paper
A pencil

What You Do

1. Draw a map of the inside of your home. Draw each door and window.
2. Mark two ways out of each room.
3. Show your map to your family. Then pick a place outside of your home where all of you can meet in case of a fire. Your safe meeting place may be a street corner or a neighbor's house.
4. Have a family fire drill once a month. Pretend the fire is in a different spot each time.

Remember to stay close to the floor. Smoke rises, so crawl underneath it, where the air is cleaner. Yell so other people know where you are. Before you open a door, touch it. If it feels hot, do not open it! Look for a different way out.

Dalmatians are known as firefighters' mascots

I N F O R M A T I O N

Index

Words to Know

bunker pants (BUN-kur pantz)—heavy, waterproof, heat-proof pants that firefighters wear while they work

calls (KALLZ)—any time the fire trucks leave the station; calls may be fires, accidents, or false alarms

dispatcher (di-SPATCH-ur)—the person who sends firefighters on calls

fire hydrants (FYR hy-drents)—large water pipes to which fire hoses are connected

turnout gear (TURN-out geer)—what firefighters wear to protect themselves from heat, smoke, and other dangers

volunteer (vah-len-TEER)—to offer to work when you do not have to; volunteers are often not paid

Read More

Maass, Rob. *Fire Fighters.* New York: Scholastic, 2002.

Masoff, Joy. *Fire!* New York: Scholastic, 2002.

Winkleman, Katherine K. *Firehouse.* New York: Walker & Co., 1994.

Internet Sites

Illinois Fire Safe Kids Page
http://www.state.il.us/kids/fire

U.S. Fire Administration Kids Page
http://www.usfa.fema.gov/kids

Sparky the Fire Dog
http://www.nfpa.org/sparky